JOURNEY
into
AFRICA

Tim Knight

OXFORD
UNIVERSITY PRESS

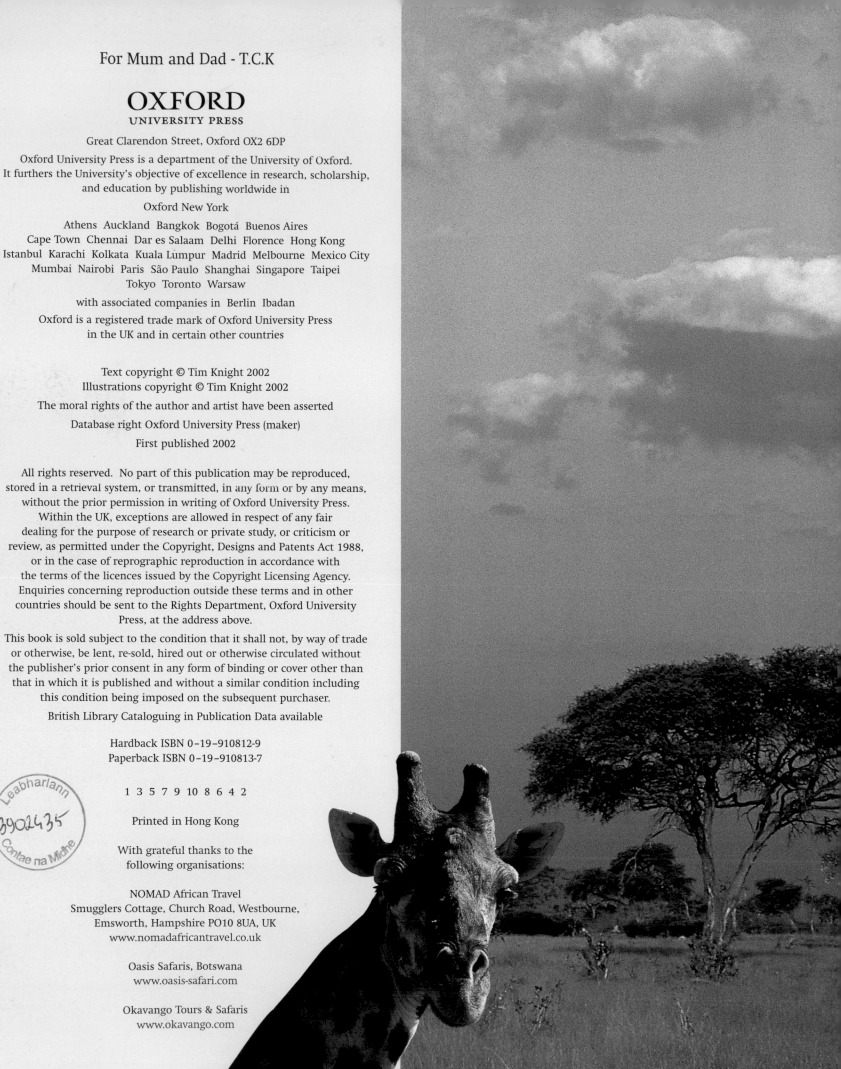

For Mum and Dad - T.C.K

OXFORD
UNIVERSITY PRESS

Great Clarendon Street, Oxford OX2 6DP

Oxford University Press is a department of the University of Oxford.
It furthers the University's objective of excellence in research, scholarship,
and education by publishing worldwide in

Oxford New York

Athens Auckland Bangkok Bogotá Buenos Aires
Cape Town Chennai Dar es Salaam Delhi Florence Hong Kong
Istanbul Karachi Kolkata Kuala Lumpur Madrid Melbourne Mexico City
Mumbai Nairobi Paris São Paulo Shanghai Singapore Taipei
Tokyo Toronto Warsaw

with associated companies in Berlin Ibadan

Oxford is a registered trade mark of Oxford University Press
in the UK and in certain other countries

Text copyright © Tim Knight 2002
Illustrations copyright © Tim Knight 2002

The moral rights of the author and artist have been asserted

Database right Oxford University Press (maker)

First published 2002

British Library Cataloguing in Publication Data available

Hardback ISBN 0–19–910812-9
Paperback ISBN 0–19–910813-7

1 3 5 7 9 10 8 6 4 2

Printed in Hong Kong

With grateful thanks to the
following organisations:

NOMAD African Travel
Smugglers Cottage, Church Road, Westbourne,
Emsworth, Hampshire PO10 8UA, UK
www.nomadafricantravel.co.uk

Oasis Safaris, Botswana
www.oasis-safari.com

Okavango Tours & Safaris
www.okavango.com

Contents

Safe
Journey!

Picture a land of vast deserts, deep lakes, thick forests, winding rivers, muddy swamps and snow-capped mountains. Imagine a place where huge elephants, lightning-quick cheetahs and sky-scraping giraffes are free to roam across the open plains. This is Africa, home to the biggest, fastest and tallest four-legged creatures on earth. An African safari is like a journey through a fantasy world. It offers the chance to meet amazing animals that we can usually see only in a zoo or on our television screens.

A wide-brimmed hat gives all-round protection against the burning sun

Binoculars help us to see animals that are far away

Dark colours blend in with the natural landscape

Long trousers and sleeves help to avoid scratches and bites

Walking boots with thick soles protect the feet from sharp rocks, thorns and snakes

► We will need to travel by canoe for part of the journey.

Going on safari is a serious business. We can make it safer and more enjoyable by being well prepared. Choosing the right clothes and equipment is very important. We need injections too, to protect us from Africa's many dangerous diseases. Insect repellent and some nasty-tasting tablets will help us to avoid catching malaria, a dangerous fever carried by mosquitoes. Swimming may not be safe. The tiny water snails found in some lakes are more dangerous than a crocodile. They carry bilharzia, a microscopic worm that can cause serious illness if it finds its way inside the human body

It's difficult to spot wildlife while playing computer games

Baseball caps cannot give full protection from the sun

◀ A four-wheel drive vehicle is essential for the rough terrain.

White is a warning colour and scares the animals

Searching for wild animals is very exciting, but we must know what to do when we meet them, especially if we are on foot. Lion cubs may look cuddly, but their parents are fierce killers. A mother elephant will even charge a truck to protect her baby. We have to be ready for anything and remember to do exactly as the guide tells us.

As long as we follow the rules, this will be a great adventure. Now that we know what to take and how to behave, let's find out more about the journey.

Leave behind the loud music and listen to the noises of Africa instead

Bare arms and legs will be cut to pieces

Designer trainers are no use on a rough safari

▲ We will need tents, mosquito nets, sleeping bags and torches at night; rucksacks, sun cream and water bottles during the day.

5

Safari Guide

Victoria falls

airstrip

village

Safari is a Swahili word. It means "long and difficult journey". In the past, this often meant a dangerous hunting trip. These days, most people go on safari to watch animals, not to shoot them. But watching animals is only part of the adventure. First, we have to find them.

Our journey will take us over steaming waterfalls, into crocodile-infested lakes, past sandy deserts and across dusty plains stretching as far as the eye can see. Travelling in Africa is hard work. In the dry season, the roads are bumpy and thick with dust. When the rains finally arrive, the tracks turn to deep, sticky mud. It is not possible to drive quickly. The best way to see animals is to camp somewhere deep in the bush, well away from busy towns, noisy people and mobile phones. When we finally reach the campsite many hours later, there will be no hot showers, flushing toilets or junk food!

Does it sound like fun to bounce around in a truck for days on end, feeling hot, tired, bruised and dirty? How about canoeing past a bad-tempered hippo? Or sneaking up on a thirsty elephant? Still interested? Let's go on safari!

river

hippo encounter

first camp

dry riverbed

lion
encounter

game
drive

bushfire

second camp

waterhole

The Smoke that Thunders

I n the distance, a long line of white smoke seems to be rising, like a huge fire stretching across the horizon. In fact, the 'smoke' is spray from one of the world's largest waterfalls. We are about to fly over Victoria Falls. The powerful Zambezi river flows through the heart of Africa. In places where hard rock and soft rock meet, the river cuts deeper into the softer rock, slowly wearing it away. At Victoria Falls, the river has carved out a spectacular cliff, 100 metres high and nearly two kilometres wide.

▶ The magnificent view through the window of a small plane makes up for the bumpy flight.

◀ Vultures have amazing eyesight. They can spot a dead animal from high above the ground.

Leaving behind the smoking waterfall, the plane passes over a huge bird. The tips of its long wings look like outstretched fingers. Gliding high above the ground, vultures make flying look easy. But getting off the ground in the first place is not quite so simple for these heavy birds. They must wait until the day warms up, so they can hitch a ride on the hot air currents that rise from the ground. Once airborne, they can spend hours soaring high in the sky, on the lookout for an easy meal.

Far below, a big, grey animal is wading into a river. Is that an elephant? Too late. The view through the window changes suddenly from muddy brown to bright blue, as the plane dips sideways. With one wing pointing skywards and the other towards the ground, we start our descent. The pilot is landing. Fasten your seat belts!

◀ In times of flood, five million cubic metres of water plunge over Victoria Falls every minute.

◀ The local name for Victoria Falls is *mosi-oa-tunya*, meaning 'smoke that thunders'.

High Noon

The plane touches down, bounces along the airstrip, and comes to a halt in a cloud of dust. A jeep is waiting nearby, ready for the long drive to our first camp. After unpacking, it is tempting to start exploring straight away, but this is no time for a long walk. The sun burns brightly overhead. Even through thick boots, the ground feels baking hot. There is plenty of shade under the big acacia trees. Beyond them lies a vast lake, whose surface dazzles in the bright sunlight.

The camp is filled with the buzzing, whining and trumpeting of insects. The most ear-splitting sound comes from the cicadas. These insects call to each other by making a very fast rattling sound, using a part of their body called a tymbal. Apart from the insect noise, there is not much sign of life. In the heat of the day, most warm-blooded animals try to keep cool by resting in the shade.

There is a loud rustling noise close by. A monitor lizard, over a metre long, scuttles out of sight behind a tree trunk. Like all reptiles, lizards spend hours sunbathing.

▲ Eye spy! Jumping spiders have excellent eyesight to help them hunt.

◄ A colourful dragonfly rests on a lakeside twig, waiting to ambush a passing insect.

Until their bodies have warmed up, they are too slow to catch food or escape their enemies. Every morning, they bask on their favourite rock, but even reptiles have to find shelter from the scorching midday sun. Most animals are active early in the morning and again in the late afternoon, when the day is cooler. Until then, the best thing to do is to find a quiet corner and join in the siesta.

► Monitor lizards will eat almost anything, from birds' eggs and small animals to rotting meat. They even swim or climb trees to find food.

Walking on Water

By late afternoon, the sun is lower in the sky. This is a perfect time to take a short boat trip and explore the edge of the lake. Animals come down to the water's edge to feed on the juicy grasses. We sit quietly in the canoe, hoping to sneak up on them. A loud snort tells the guide that a buffalo is feeding nearby. He paddles away quickly. It is wise to keep a safe distance from a bad-tempered buffalo.

▶ A jacana walks across the lake's surface, using the floating leaves for support.

▼ Crocodiles have lived on Earth since the time of the dinosaurs.

Beyond the reed bed, a crocodile is lying on the muddy bank. Its huge mouth is wide open. A small bird lands on the crocodile's nose, then hops inside its mouth and begins pecking among the teeth, picking out bits of food. The crocodile allows its visitor to continue feeding. It has learned that a walking toothbrush is more useful than a bird-sized snack.

▲ A green carpet of water lilies bursts into flower on the water's surface.

▶ Who's been sleeping in my reed-bed? A cattle egret settles down for the night.

We drift on through a patch of water lily leaves, called lily pads. A jacana bird is using them as stepping stones. Jacanas are also known as lily-trotters, because their long toes and enormous feet help them to walk on the floating plants. As the sun goes down, the guide paddles back towards the camp. Birds are starting to gather in flocks among the reeds for the night. This keeps them safe from night-time hunters.

Call of the
Wild

An African sunset is an unforgettable sight. Some evenings the whole sky glows bright orange, as though it is on fire.

► Camping in Africa is a great adventure, but some people prefer to sleep in a comfortable lodge!

At dusk, when the sun has just disappeared below the horizon, biting insects such as mosquitoes start to appear. Some female *Anopheles* mosquitoes carry malaria, a dangerous tropical disease. In the evening, it is best to use insect repellent and wear trousers and long-sleeved shirts to avoid being bitten. Back at camp, we eat a tasty supper of chicken and rice, cooked on an open fire. Everyone is tired.

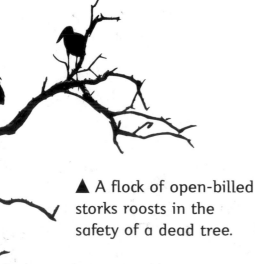

▲ A flock of open-billed storks roosts in the safety of a dead tree.

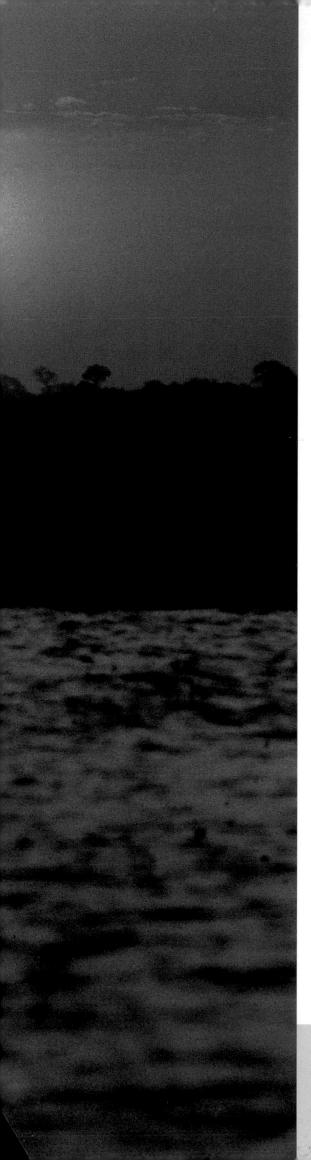

Before long we are all safely tucked up in our sleeping bags, under a mosquito net. After zipping up the tent flaps to keep out scorpions and snakes, we lie back and gaze out through the tent window. There are no lights in the middle of the African bush, so the stars are much brighter there. It looks as though a giant diamond has exploded into a million pieces, showering the night sky with brilliant jewels.

Somewhere in the darkness, an owl hoots. There is a rustling outside the tent. The creatures of the night are stirring. We fall asleep with the bleeping and croaking of a thousand frogs ringing in our ears. Later, a rumbling noise wakes the whole camp. At first, it sounds like distant thunder. As it draws closer, it turns into a loud roar, so close to the tent that the ground seems to shake. Silence. Even the frogs seem to be listening. But the roaring has stopped. The visitor has already left.

▲ Unlike most owls, the pearl-spotted owl is often seen during daylight.

◄ The sun sets behind a herd of grazing buffalo.

► A painted reed frog, smaller than a man's thumbnail, flattens itself against a plant stem.

The Early Bird

Before the first light of dawn, the noises of the night have already faded away. Now the air is filled instead with squawking, whistling and shrieking, as birds and monkeys start to wake up. Africa is no place for those who like a lie-in. There is a feeling of excitement in the camp. Someone heard lions roaring during the night. So that's what it was! The jeep's engine is already running. We're off to look for lions.

Our guide, Cisco, drives slowly, stopping regularly to check the ground for animal footprints. Could one of those sandy rocks in the distance be a sleeping lion? It is a dusty ride, because there has been no rain for many months. Most of the rivers have disappeared too. We reach a steep bank. During last year's rains there was a raging torrent here, too deep for a vehicle to cross. Now there is only a dry riverbed.

▲ Although a giraffe's neck is incredibly long, it has just seven bones connecting its head to its body, the same number as humans.

Among the nearby acacia trees, a few branches are shaking. A long-necked, spindly-legged creature is tugging at a mouthful of leaves high in the tree-tops. Adult giraffes are taller than a telegraph pole and can reach the highest branches. A giraffe needs a very big heart to pump blood all the way to its head. Its tongue is as rough as sandpaper, so it has no problem chewing the sharp acacia thorns.

▶ An acacia tree grows sharp thorns to protect its leaves.

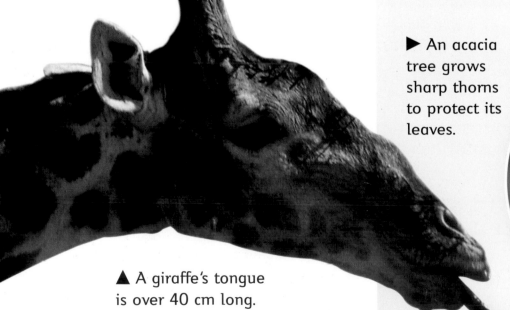

▲ A giraffe's tongue is over 40 cm long.

▲ The lilac-breasted roller is the national bird of Botswana.

▲ A baby zebra can recognise its mother by the pattern of her stripes.

A bird with beautiful, rainbow-coloured feathers calls loudly from its perch in a dead tree. A second bird flies overhead, diving and rolling in mid-air. Like fighter pilots showing off, these lilac-breasted rollers are displaying to each other above their territory, the place where they have made a home.

A herd of relaxed-looking zebras watch the vehicle for a few moments, before continuing to graze on the dry grass. They would be more nervous if the lions were close by. Zebras may all look the same to us, but each one has a different stripe pattern, as unique as a human fingerprint. When it feeds among bushes or long grass, a zebra is surprisingly hard to see, because its stripes help to disguise the shape of its body.

▲ Walking with heads upside down, flamingos use their beaks like a sieve to collect their microscopic food.

Let's Stick
Together

Zebras are not the only animals that live in large groups. Birds come together for food as well as safety. Millions of flamingos gather on lakes and salt pans to feed on tiny algae, the miniature plants that grow in the water. Seen from a distance, a flamingo flock looks like a giant pink stain spreading through the water, as though someone has spilt the world's biggest pot of paint.

► Early warning system. A female impala keeps watch while others feed.

A herd of impalas, a common type of antelope, is grazing quietly nearby. They don't all feed at once. Some of them look around nervously, and snort loudly at the slightest sign of danger. With so many ears, eyes and noses on red alert, the herd is unlikely to be taken by surprise. Even if a lion or cheetah attacks, each impala has a better chance of escaping as part of a big group.

Animals that hunt, called predators, sometimes stick together too. Wild dogs hunt in packs. When they chase an antelope herd, they look closely for a weak or injured animal. Once they spot one, they take turns snapping at its heels and biting it until it is too tired to run any further. With their needle-sharp teeth, a pack of wild dogs can eat a whole antelope in five minutes.

We spot a thorn tree nearby that is full of birds' nests. These belong to weavers, sparrow-like birds that often live in large, noisy colonies. They build their nests by weaving and knotting together pieces of grass. An expert can tell what kind of weaver lives in a colony just by looking at the shape of the nests.

◄ Safety in numbers. A colony of buffalo weavers in an overcrowded tree.

► Leader of the pack. A wild dog prepares for the hunt after a long rest.

Campfire
Stories

Back in camp, as darkness falls, a hamerkop flies back to its treetop nest. Many tribes believe it is a bird of ill omen, bringing bad luck to those who see it. Some will even burn down their house if a hamerkop flies over it. Most stories are spoken out loud, not written down. Cisco tells us the hippopotamus story that he first heard from his grandfather:

At first the other animals did not want the hippo to live in the river, because they thought he would eat all the fish. To prove to them that he only ate grass, the hippo promised to spray his dung on to the bushes whenever he came out of the water, so that they could check it for signs of fish bones!

▼ A hippo can eat up to 60kg of grass in a single night.

▲ The puff adder is responsible for three-quarters of all snakebite injuries in Africa.

'Hippopotamus' is a strange word, but it just means 'river horse'. Animal and plant names come from different languages. When Dutch farmers settled in Africa, they named the hamerkop after the shape of its head. In their language, Afrikaans, hamerkop means 'hammer head'. Once we have seen a shoebill, a sausage tree, or a bat-eared fox, funny names make more sense.

During supper, Cisco tells stories about Africa's dangerous snakes. He talks about the deadly spitting cobra, which spits poison to defend itself, aiming at the eyes. We shiver as he describes the giant, 6 metre-long pythons that can squeeze a large antelope to death and swallow it whole. Finally, we hear that the highly poisonous puff adder likes to crawl inside warm sleeping bags. This could be a sleepless night!

▲ A
us t

You Scratch My Back...

As we leave behind the disgruntled hippo, we pass a hamerkop at the water's edge. This bird often shares its home with a deadly snake. The cool, dark inside of a hamerkop nest is the perfect place for a black mamba to sleep. Mambas eat mainly rats, so the bird is in no danger, but its uninvited guest will frighten away any nest robbers. The snake is not just a lodger. It is a bodyguard and childminder too.

Nearby, a male warthog is rolling in the mud. Wallowing like this helps him to keep cool and the coat of mud protects his skin from biting insects and blood-sucking spiders called ticks.

Ticks feed by cutting a hole in the skin, sticking in their tiny snout, and drinking the blood like lemonade through a straw. Creatures that feed on other animals are called parasites. Their victims are known as hosts. Mud wallows and dust baths are not the only way to remove parasites. Monkeys comb through each others' fur, using their fingers to pick off anything nasty. This is known as mutual grooming.

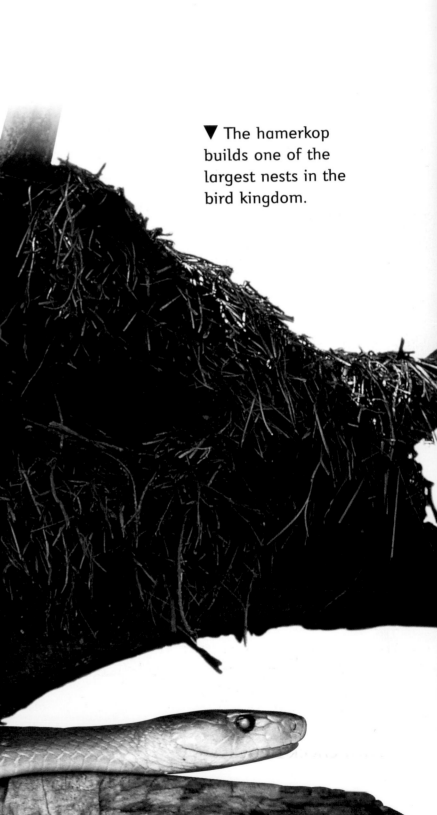

▼ The hamerkop builds one of the largest nests in the bird kingdom.

▼ The aggressive black mamba is the most feared snake in Africa.

24   26

▲ Cattle egrets often follow a grazing buffalo, and feed on the insects disturbed by its hooves.

▶ Yellow-billed oxpeckers enjoying a movable feast.

Others use a different kind of pest control. Oxpeckers, distant cousins of the starling, have learnt to hitch a ride on animals and climb all over them in search of a meal. Through binoculars, we can see them clinging to a zebra's back, using their stiff tails to balance as they peck out the fat ticks. The oxpeckers use the zebra as a walking restaurant. In return, the zebra gets a free health check from its very own team of flying doctors.

King of the
Beasts

Around the very first bend, Cisco suddenly stops the truck. Lying in the shade, panting to cool down, is a huge lion. His magnificent golden mane is already turning black in places. Although he looks tired he is in his prime, as fit and as strong as he will ever be.

◀ A lioness relaxes with her daughters.

A growling noise behind the truck makes us turn around. A whole group of lions, called a pride, is walking out of the bushes. There are five adult females, called lionesses, two young males and half a dozen cubs of different ages. A lioness leads the way. She is the matriarch, the most important female who keeps the pride in order. She yawns widely, showing the strong, sharp teeth that are so important for killing and eating. Once a lion loses its teeth, or has its jaw broken by a kick from a zebra, it will die of starvation.

A noisy flock of vultures begins fighting over the half-eaten buffalo carcass abandoned by the lions. Vultures and other scavengers like marabou storks, jackals and hyenas are quick to arrive when lions make a kill. The big male lions always eat first. Everyone else must wait their turn. This is called a pecking order. The brave or impatient ones try to sneak in and steal a quick mouthful. A large clan of hungry hyenas may even drive off the lions before they have finished eating. Their jaws are strong enough to break up the skin and bones of any animal, even an elephant. Hyenas are like dustbins on legs. They eat almost anything, dead or alive.

▲ The marabou stork's beak is strong enough to puncture the hide of a dead buffalo.

▼ Vultures with no table manners squabble over the remains of a lion kill.

◀ Lion cubs are often left alone while the pride is hunting.

31

Mobile Homes

In the morning, the lions have moved on. It's time for us to do the same. Some animals have permanent homes. For others, home is wherever they can find food. These nomadic animals wander far and wide in search of fresh grass. Wherever they go, the predators must follow.

Outside the towns and villages, Africa still has many nomadic groups, people who move from place to place. Some grow crops. Others keep cattle or goats, on which they depend for meat, milk, cheese and clothing. These nomads live in temporary huts, made from mud, stones and grass, until it is time to search for fresh water or new grazing land for their animals. Some even carry their homes with them when they leave.

Elephants searching for water have scraped this baobab tree trunk with their tusks.

We make our new camp near a tree that seems to be growing upside down. The baobab, or 'upside down tree', is very important to the Bushmen. They turn its fruit into sweets and make musical instruments from the wood. Best of all, its trunk is swollen with precious water.

As we collect wood for the fire, a small bird appears and starts calling. It's a honeyguide. While Cisco is preparing lunch, he tells us how the honeyguide and the Bushman help each other. Like partners in crime, they rob bees' nests together and then split the loot. The bird guides the Bushman to the nest with its 'follow me' call, and waits for him to smoke out the bees. The man takes most of the honey, leaving part of the honeycomb for the bird, which eats the bees' grubs and wax. Bushmen believe that any honeyguide not given its share will lead the next person straight to a dangerous animal instead!

In the Kalahari Desert of southern Africa, the Bushmen survive without keeping animals. Their ancestors have lived off the land for thousands of years. They hunt with spears, find fruit, dig up roots or gather grass seed for food. Bushmen have learned which plants are safe to eat and which are poisonous. They can also find water even in the hottest, driest places.

▶ Hunter-gatherers like these Bushmen are experts at catching animals for food.

Glossary

Acacia Thorny tree with feathery leaves eaten by a variety of animals

Algae Miniature plants found in water

Baboon Large monkey with long, sharp teeth

Baobab Huge tree with a fat, water-filled trunk

Bat-eared fox Fox that hunts at night by using its large ears to listen for food

Bilharzia Tiny worm, found in water-snails and dangerous to humans

Bush Area of wild, open spaces well away from towns and villages

Bushmen Small, nomadic huntsmen from southern Africa

Camouflage Disguise that helps an animal to hide

Carcass Dead animal

Cicada Noisy insect that calls loudly to find a mate

Clan Large group of hyenas

Drought Long period without rain

Egret Type of heron, usually with white feathers

Gnu Another name for a wildebeest

Gregarious Living in large flocks or herds

Grooming Keeping fur clean by removing dirt and parasites

Hamerkop Bird with a hammer-shaped head, famous for its enormous nest

Hide Skin of an animal

Honeyguide Type of bird that guides men to bees' nests

Host Plant or animal on which a parasite feeds or lives

Impala Common type of antelope found throughout Africa

Ivory Hard, white material such as elephant tusks

Jacana Water-bird with enormous feet

Klipspringer Small antelope that lives on steep cliffs

Malaria Disease carried by some mosquitoes, causing fever or even death

Mamba Large, deadly, fast-moving African snake

Marabou Large stork that mainly eats dead meat

Matriarch Female leader of a large family of animals

Migration Long journey from one home to another

Monitor Type of very large lizard

Nomadic Moving from one area to another, rather than always living in the same place

Oxpecker Bird that eats the parasites found on cattle and wild animals

Parasite Plant or animal that feeds on another living plant or animal

Poacher Illegal hunter who kills animals, often for money

Predator Animal that hunts and kills other animals

Prey Animal that is killed and eaten by a predator

Pride Family of lions

Puff adder Poisonous snake that puffs out its body when disturbed

Python Large non-poisonous snake that kills by crushing its prey

Roller Brightly coloured, acrobatic bird

Safari Swahili word for "journey"

Salt pan Large area of salt left behind after water evaporates

Sausage Tree Tree with red, bell-shaped flowers and huge sausage-shaped fruit

Scavenger Animal that eats scraps and rotten food such as dead meat

Shoebill Large, uncommon stork with a massive bill, also known as the whale-head

Swahili Language spoken in parts of East Africa

Talon Hooked claw

Termite Tiny insect that eats dead plants

Tick Blood-sucking spider that feeds on warm-blooded animals

Troop Large family of monkeys

Tsessebe Large, fast-running antelope

Tymbal Part of a cicada's body, used to produce a loud noise

Waterhole Pool of water where animals gather to drink

Weaver Type of bird that builds a nest woven from grass or twigs

Index

Acknowledgements

All photos Tim Knight, except:
Planet Earth/Steve Bloom, front cover c; Richard Clemence, pages 4/5 (children); Estée Knight, page 10, page 14 (circle), page 41 (circle); Anthony Bannister, © Gallo Images/CORBIS page 35br; John Gosler map artwork page 6.
Additional thanks to: Aaron Chan; Sophie Conlon; Jessica Creak; Oriel Southwood; Harry Steyn; YHA Adventure Shops, Oxford.